A TIME FOR TROLLS
FAIRY TALES FROM NORWAY

A TIME
FOR TROLLS

FAIRY TALES FROM NORWAY

TOLD BY
ASBJÖRNSEN
AND MOE

+

SELECTED AND TRANSLATED
WITH AN INTRODUCTION
BY JOAN ROLL-HANSEN

ILLUSTRATIONS BY
HANS GERHARD SÖRENSEN

TANUM - NORLI - OSLO

This translation first published 1962
Third edition 1964
Reprinted 1965, 1966, 1967, 1969, 1970, 1972, 1974, 1977, 1982

© JOAN ROLL-HANSEN 1962

Illustrations by Hans Gerhard Sörensen

Dreyer Aksjeselskap

ISBN 82-518-0081-1

CONTENTS

INTRODUCTION

The farmers and forest workers who told or listened to these tales had no contact with courtly life. In the period when the folk tales flourished, Norway was ruled from Denmark and the King had his permanent court in Copenhagen. So the fairy tale king and his residence are envisaged in terms of the experience of the isolated farming communities in the Norwegian valleys. The king is portrayed as a prosperous farmer, with neighbours of the same degree. The royal hall of residence (Norwegian "kongsgaarden") is seen as a large, sturdily timbered farm-house, flanked by outhouses. The king himself stands on the steps of his porch, supervising with a shrewd eye the working of his wealthy farming estate, with its fields and forests and rocky hills.

In this setting we meet the hero Askelad, who is a kind of Norwegian Aladdin. He is no grand figure. The qualities that make him deserve his princess and his share of the kingdom lie beneath the surface. He is slow to take action, but acts with insight once he gets started. His early life is spent in apparent idleness, tending the fire and raking the ashes. Hence his name, Askelad, the "lad of the ashes". A boy Cinderella, he sits by his fireside and gradually develops keen powers of observation, led on by his curiosity in a world he finds rich and strange. He is prepared to cultivate his modest skills patiently and diligently. His two elder brothers swagger along through life, confident of quick success, and fail to notice the things that would bring them real happiness. They turn up their noses at an old baking-trough, a nail or a stump of candle. But Askelad can put all these things to good use in order to trick the troll and make off with the treasure. And his wonder at the odd noises of a forest can lead him to a magic axe which he keeps with care. It is his willingness to commune with the world and gather small experiences that strengthens his hidden powers, his steadfastness, his humour, his quick wits.

Kindness to man and beast is practised by Askelad. But in none of the tales does the code of kindness apply to the supernatural creatures who are hostile to the human race. The devil and the trolls are fair game. Without any qualms of conscience Askelad makes a stew of the troll's daughter. The Big Billikin Whiskers triumphantly dashes the river troll to pieces. In the folk consciousness, the trolls are associated with the dangerous, blind forces of nature. They are pictured as enormous, clumsy creatures, often many-headed, and stupid, in spite of their extraordinary strength and magic powers. As in Norse mythology, they are thought of as the guardians of gold and silver and mineral wealth.

The most boisterous version of the peasant hero appears in the comic tale, "Rumble-Mumble Goose-Egg", a grand piece of jest in which fairy tale conventions are mocked. Rumble-Mumble is a changeling, with elements of troll, animal, and man, who in the course of his adventures matures into a figure like Askelad. To begin with he has tremendous strength but little sense, though he is well-meaning, and only knocks the life out of a dozen farm workers when he is hungry and impatient for his meal. His basic desire is to work well and he uses his great strength to serve the kingdom. Gradually his experiences make him acquire quick senses and sure skills, his efforts move in a more positive direction, and in the end he can outwit the troll and the devil and the ungrateful king.

These tales also have many themes in common with fairy tales from other lands. There is the theme of the grateful beasts. In return for help in distress, the beasts grant the hero protection and also endow him with the special wits and courage of the animal world. The generous daughter in "The Two Stepsisters" is helped by the little birds to win the witch's treasure, and all the creatures she has assisted protect her during her escape. In another tale, the lion, the falcon and the ant grant the hero the power to assume their shape, and he is then able to gain secret knowledge of the life force of the giant trolls and destroy them all.

Much of the symbolism will also be familiar from other Euro-

pean tales and legends. In "East of the Sun and West of the Moon" we recognise a version of the Greek legend of Cupid and Psyche, with the theme of the maturing of love through a painful search. "The Seven Foals" has features from the medieval legend of the Holy Grail, with the theme of spiritual regeneration in the lonely chapel and the vestiges of ancient fertility ritual mingled with Christian ceremony. Both these tales celebrate the triumph of Christianity over witchcraft and paganism.

Norwegian folk tales were not collected and written down until the middle of the nineteenth century. In 1837 two young student friends, P. C. Asbjörnsen and Jörgen Moe, decided to prepare the first collections for publication. What the brothers Grimm had done in the field of German folk tales, they wished to do in Norway. But they were both convinced that the style of the Grimm fairy tales was too ornate and literary. They agreed that their versions ought to be written in a popular style, as close to that of the originals as possible, with all the colloquialism, the verve, the ripe humour of the tales that were living in the woods and valleys. At the same time, they wished to avoid using marked local dialects that might not be understood in the rest of Norway. Their great achievement was to create, in close co-operation, a style in which these aims were carried out. Norwegian popular speech appeared in writing for the first time. Often several local versions of a tale were welded into a master version which still preserved the true spirit and raciness of the originals.

From 1841 to 1871 their versions of the folk tales, "Norske Folkeeventyr", continued to appear. Both Asbjörnsen and Moe showed a remarkable dedication to this task. They had little encouragement and little money. They had to give time to other careers for a living: Asbjörnsen became an inspector of forests, Jörgen Moe a clergyman. They were sustained by the joy they had felt in childhood when they first heard the tales. They were both able to make contact with humble folk and gain their confidence, Jörgen Moe being the son of a farmer and Asbjörnsen the son of a glazier in Kristiania. They knew best the tales from the woods north of the Oslo fjord. Later they travelled in many of the valleys of South Norway gathering more material, and they had *material sent by post, at their own expense, from clergymen and friends in more remote districts. Each developed an individual vein. Asbjörnsen had a lively imagination, a full-blooded spontaneity and verve, and excelled in humorous tales. He also collected legends and "hulder" tales. Jörgen Moe had a more highly developed sense of form and was a master at rendering the more serious, epic tales. He collected folk songs and ballads and also wrote lyric poetry.*

The publication of "Norske Folkeeventyr" had a far-reaching effect on the Norwegian national consciousness. At a time of general national revival, it meant a great deal for national self-respect to discover that during the dark years of Danish domination the unlettered folk of Norway had fostered such a rich store of powerful tales. The linguistic and imaginative impact upon Norwegian literature was very strong. Ibsen steeped himself in the tales. His great tragic drama, "Peer Gynt", draws on the language and content of both fairy tale and legend. Peer Gynt fancies himself as a fairy tale hero, but his tragedy is that he imagines he can win happiness the easy way.

In choosing these tales from the folk collections of Asbjörnsen and Moe, I have tried to make a representative selection and also to avoid tales that have appeared recently in English translation.

Oslo, January 1962

Joan Roll-Hansen

ASKELAD
AND
THE SILVER DUCKS

There was once a poor man who had three sons. When he died, the two eldest sons went out into the world to seek their fortune, but they would not let the youngest son go with them. "We know what you're fit for!" they said. "All you do is squat by the fire, fiddling with the ashes."

"I'll go alone, then," said Askelad.

The two eldest brothers walked off and made their way to the king's farm. There they entered into service, one under the stable groom and one under the gardener. Askelad started out too and took with him a big kneading-trough, the only thing their parents had left them. The other brothers had not cared about it and it was heavy to carry, but he did not like to leave it behind. After walking a while, he also came to the king's farm and asked for service. They told him they did not need him, still he kept on asking so politely that in the end he was allowed to help in the kitchen and carry wood and water for the cook. He was quick and willing to work, and soon he was well liked by everyone there. But the two other brothers were lazy and got blows by the dozen and little wages. And they grew envious of Askelad when they saw him doing so well.

Opposite the king's farm, on the other side of a big lake, there lived a troll who had seven silver ducks. These ducks basked and swam on the lake and they could be seen from the king's farm. The king had often wished they were his, and one day the two eldest brothers said to the groom, "If our brother liked, he could easily get the seven silver ducks for the king. He has said so." And you can be sure the groom lost no time in passing this on to the king. Then the king called in Askelad and said to him, "Your brothers tell me you are willing to get me those silver ducks. Go and get them now."

"I've never thought of such a thing," said the lad.

But the king was not to be put off. "You've said you'll do it," he said, "and I'm going to take you at your word, my lad."

"Well," said the lad, "if there's no way out of it, please let me have a quarter of rye and a quarter of wheat, and I'll try and get them." He was given the rye and the wheat and he stored it in the kneading-trough he had brought from home, and in this he rowed across the lake. After he reached the other side, he walked along the shore scattering the grain. At last he was able to lure the ducks inside his trough, and then he rowed back as fast as he could.

When he got to the middle of the lake, the troll came out and saw him.

"Have you made off with my seven silver ducks?" he shouted.

"I have," said the lad.

"Will you be coming again?" asked the troll.

"I might," said the lad.

When he came back to the king with the seven silver ducks, he became even more popular in the household and the king himself gave him praise. But his brothers grew more sullen and jealous, and they decided to tell the groom that Askelad had said he could get the king the troll's quilt with all the checks of silver and gold, any time at all. And the groom wasted no time in telling the king this news. Then the king spoke to the lad, and told him he knew from his brothers that he had boasted of being able to get hold of the troll's quilt with the silver and gold checks. Now he was to do so, or pay with his life. Askelad replied that he had never said any such thing. But it was no use, and so he asked for three days to find a plan. Three days later, he rowed across the lake again in his kneading-trough and walked about keeping careful watch. At last he caught sight of the hill-folk putting out the quilt to air it. And as soon as they disappeared inside the mountain, Askelad seized the quilt and rowed back as fast as he could.

When he was out in the middle of the lake, the troll came along and saw him.

"Didn't you steal my seven silver ducks"? shouted the troll.

"Yes, I did," said the lad.

"And have you just stolen my quilt with all the checks of silver and gold?"

"I have," said the lad.

"Will you be coming here again?"

"I might," said the lad.

When he returned with the gold and silver quilt, he became even more popular, and he was made the king's personal servant. This made the other brothers much more vexed, and in revenge they agreed to say to the groom, "Our brother has told us that he can get the king the troll's golden harp. This harp makes everyone glad when they hear it, no matter how sad they are."

And the groom went straight to the king and told him the news, and the king said to the lad, "I'm going to take you at your word again. If you get me the harp, I'll give you my daughter and half my kingdom. If you don't, you'll pay with your life."

"I've never thought or said any such thing," replied Askelad. "But I suppose there's no choice and I'd better try. Could you let me have six days to find a plan?" The six days were granted and when they were over he had to set out. He took with him in his pocket a nail, a birch-twig, and a candle-end, and rowed across the lake. Near the mountain he started pacing quickly to and fro. And after a while the troll came out and saw him.

"Didn't you steal my seven silver ducks?" shouted the troll.

"I did," said the lad.

"And didn't you steal my quilt with the silver and gold checks as well?"

"Yes, I did," said the lad.

Then the troll seized him and carried him inside the mountain. "Well, daughter," he said. 'Now I've caught the boy who stole my silver ducks and my quilt with the checks of silver and gold. Fatten him up and we can kill him and invite our friends to a feast." She set to work at once and put him in the fattening pen. And he was there for eight days, and was given the best food and drink, as much as he wanted.

After eight days had passed, the troll told his daughter to go and cut his little finger to find out whether he was fat enough.

She went down to the fattening pen. "Give me your little finger," she said. But Askelad offered her the nail he had brought with him and she cut that.

"Oh, he's still as hard as nails," said the troll's daughter when she came in to her father. "He's not ready yet."

Eight days later the same thing happened, only this time Askelad held out the birch-twig. "He's a bit better," she said when she came back to her father. "But he's still as tough as wood."

But after eight days more, the troll told his daughter to go out again and see whether he was fat enough yet. "Give me your little finger!" said the troll's daughter to Askelad in the fattening pen. And this time he let her have the candle-end.

14

"I think he's fair enough now," she said.

"Oh, is he?" said the troll. "I'll be off then and invite our guests. In the meantime you can kill him and roast one half of him and boil the other."

After the troll had gone, the daughter began to sharpen a long, long knife.

"Are you going to use that to slaughter me?" asked the lad.

"Yes, my lad!" said the troll's daughter.

"But the blade's not keen enough," said the lad. "I can sharpen it for you, and then it will be all the easier for you to kill me."

And she gave him the knife, and he started to whet the blade.

"Let me try it on your hair," said the lad. "It should be just right now." And she let him do so. But as he took her by the hair he bent back her neck and cut off her head. Then he boiled half of her and roasted the other half and set the dish on the table. And he dressed himself in her clothes and sat down in a far corner.

When the troll came home with his guests, he thought it was his daughter sitting there and asked her to come and join them at their meal.

"No," answered the lad. "I don't want anything to eat. I feel out of sorts."

"Well, you know how to raise your spirits," said the troll. "Play upon our golden harp."

"Oh, yes! Where is it again?" asked Askelad.

"You know well enough. You had it last. It's hanging up there over the door!" said the troll.

Askelad did not need to be told twice. He took down the harp and wandered in and out playing upon it. But all of a sudden he pushed his kneading-trough out on the lake and rowed off so fast that the waters swirled about him.

After a while the troll thought his daughter had been away a long time and he went out to see what was the matter. Then he caught sight of the lad in his trough far out in the middle of the lake.

"Aren't you the one who stole my seven silver ducks?" shouted

the troll.

"Yes," said Askelad.

"And didn't you steal my quilt with the silver and gold checks as well?"

"Yes," said Askelad.

"Have you just taken my golden harp?" cried the troll.

"Yes, I have," said the lad.

"Haven't I eaten you up, then?"

"No! You've eaten your daughter," answered the lad.

And when the troll heard this, he became so angry that he burst. So then Askelad rowed back to the mountain and carried away a heap of gold and silver, as much as he could store in his trough. After he returned to the king's farm with the golden harp, he wedded the princess and got half the kingdom, just as the king had promised. But he was good to his brothers, for he believed that they had only meant well when they spoke of him in the household.

THE THREE
BILLIKIN WHISKERS

Once upon a time there were three billy-goats who were on their way to the mountain grass to get fat, and each of them was called Billikin Whiskers. As they walked along they had to cross a bridge over a waterfall, and under the bridge there lived a big, horrid troll with eyes like pewter plates and a nose as long as a rake-handle.

First the youngest Billikin Whiskers came to cross the bridge.

Trip, trip, trip, trip, went the bridge.

"Who's that tripping over my bridge?" roared the troll.

"Oh, I'm the smallest Billikin Whiskers, and I'm on my way to the mountain grass to get fat," said the billy-goat, in a tiny, tiny voice.

"Now I'm coming to eat you up!" said the troll.

"Oh no! Don't eat me up. I'm so small. Wait a while, till the second Billikin Whiskers comes. He's much bigger."

"Very well," said the troll.

A little while later the second Billikin Whiskers came to cross the bridge.

Trot, trot, trot, trot, went the bridge.

"Who's that trotting over my bridge?" roared the troll.

"Oh, I'm the second Billikin Whiskers on my way to the mountain grass to get fat," said the billy-goat, in a clear, clear voice.

"Now I'm coming to eat you up!" said the troll.

"Oh no! Don't eat me up. Wait a while, till the big Billikin Whiskers comes. He's much, much bigger."

"Very well, then," said the troll.

And all of a sudden, the big Billikin Whiskers came along.

Tramp, tramp, tramp, tramp, went the bridge. He was so heavy that the bridge creaked and groaned under him.

"Who's that tramping over my bridge?" roared the troll.

"I'm the BIG Billikin Whiskers!" said the billy-goat in a deep, deep voice.

"Now I'm coming to eat you up!" roared the troll.

"Up you come! I have two spears!
With them I'll tear your eyes and ears.
I have two mighty boulder-stones!
With them I'll crush your marrow and bones,"
said the billy-goat. And he charged at the troll and stuck out his eyes, and battered his marrow and bones, and butted him over the edge of the waterfall. And then he went up to the mountain grass. There the billy-goats got so fat, so very, very fat, that they could hardly walk home again. And as far as I know, they are still as fat as that.

And this is the end of my tale.

THE MAN
WHO KEPT HOUSE

There was once a cross and peevish man who had the idea that his wife never did enough in the house. One evening he came home from the haymaking, swearing and grumbling like a bear with a sore head.

"Oh, my dear, don't scold so!" said his wife. "Tomorrow we'll change jobs. I'll go out with the haymakers and you can do the housework."

The man liked this plan well enough and said he was willing.

Early next morning the wife shouldered the scythe and went out into the meadow to cut hay, and the man set about working in the house. First he thought he would churn butter, but after churning a while he felt thirsty and went down to the cellar to tap ale. While he was tapping ale into a bowl, he heard the pig wander into the house. He darted up the cellar steps with the tap in his hand to get to the pig before it could upset the churn. But when he found the churn knocked over and the pig gobbling up the cream now spilt all over floor, he flew into such a rage that he clean forgot about the barrel of ale and made a bee-line for the pig. He caught up with it in the doorway and gave it a stout kick, so that it never stirred again. Then it dawned on him that he still had the tap in his hand, but by the time he reached the cellar the barrel was dry.

He set out for the milk-shed once more and found enough cream to fill the churn and kept on churning away, for he wanted to have butter ready for dinner. After he had been churning a while, he suddenly remembered that there was a cow at home in the stable still without a thing to eat or drink at this late hour. It seemed too far take her to the field, and he thought he might as well put her to graze on the roof, there being a turf roof on the farm-house with thick, rich grass. The house was on a steep hillside and he was sure he could get the cow up on the roof without mishap if he laid a plank across. But he did not dare let go of the churn either, for fear of it being upset by the baby who was crawling about on all fours. So he hoisted the churn on his back and went out to water the cow before he led her up to the roof. He seized a bucket to fetch water from the well, but when he bent over the side of the well to draw up the water the cream poured out of the churn and ran down his neck.

It was getting on for dinner-time, and he still had no butter. So he thought he had better make porridge and hung a pot of water over the hearth. Then it crossed his mind that the cow might fall off the roof and break her legs or her neck, and so he went up to tether her safely. He tied a loop round the cow's neck, slipped the rope down through the chimney, and tied the other end round his own leg, for the water was already boiling in the pot and he had to start mixing the porridge. While he was doing so, the cow did fall off the roof after all and pulled the man up the chimney by the leg. There he got stuck, and the cow outside was in a fine pickle, dangling beside the wall, neither up nor down.

The wife had been waiting hour after hour for the man to come and call her in to dinner, but time dragged on and nothing happened. At last she grew weary and started for home. As soon as she caught sight of the unhappy cow hanging there, she went up to it and cut the rope with her scythe. Then the man fell down the chimney, and when the wife came in he was standing on his head in the porridge pot.

THE COCK
AND THE HEN
IN THE HAZELWOOD

Once upon a time the cock and the hen went into the hazelwood to pick nuts.

And the hen got a nutshell stuck in her throat and she lay there flapping her wings. The cock wanted to fetch water for her, and he ran off to the spring and said: "Dear spring, give me water to give to Hickety, my dear hen, who is fighting for her life in the hazelwood."

The spring answered: "You'll get no water till you bring me leaves."

And the cock ran off to the lime-tree: "Dear lime-tree, give me leaves to give to the spring, who will give me water to give to Hickety, my dear hen, who is fighting for her life in the hazelwood."

"You'll get no leaves till you bring me ribbons of red gold," answered the lime-tree.

And the cock ran off to the Virgin Mary: "Dear Virgin Mary, give me ribbons of red gold to give to the lime-tree, who will give me leaves to give to the spring, who will give me water to give to Hickety, my dear hen, who is fighting for her life in the hazelwood."

"You'll get no ribbons of red gold till you bring me shoes," answered the Virgin Mary.

And the cock ran off to the shoemaker: "Dear shoemaker, give me shoes to give to the Virgin Mary, who will give me ribbons of red gold to give to the lime-tree, who will give me leaves to give to the spring, who will give me water to give to Hickety, my dear hen, who is fighting for her life in the hazelwood."

"You'll get no shoes till you bring me bristles," answered the
shoemaker.

And the cock ran off to the sow: "Dear sow, give me bristles to give to the shoemaker, who will give me shoes to give to the Virgin Mary, who will give me ribbons of red gold to give to the lime-tree, who will give me leaves to give to the spring, who will give me water to give to Hickety, my dear hen, who is fighting for her life in the hazelwood."

"You'll get no bristles till you bring me corn," answered the sow.

And the cock ran off to the thresher: "Dear thresher, give me corn to give to the sow, who will give me bristles to give to the shoemaker, who will give me shoes to give to the Virgin Mary, who will give me ribbons of red gold to give to the lime-tree, who will give me leaves to give to the spring, who will give me water to give to Hickety, my dear hen, who is fighting for her life in the hazelwood."

"You'll get no corn till you bring me a bannock," answered the thresher.

And the cock ran off to the bakeress: "Dear bakeress, give me a bannock to give to the thresher, who will give me corn to give to the sow, who will give me bristles to give to the shoemaker, who will give me shoes to give to the Virgin Mary, who will give me ribbons of red gold to give to the lime-tree, who will give me leaves to give to the spring, who will give me water to give to Hickety, my dear hen, who is fighting for her life in the hazelwood.

"You'll get no bannock till you bring me wood," answered the bakeress.

And the cock ran off to the woodcutter: "Dear woodcutter, give me wood to give to the bakeress, who will give me a bannock to give to the thresher, who will give me corn to give to the sow, who will give me bristles to give to the shoemaker, who will give me shoes to give to the Virgin Mary, who will give me ribbons of red gold to give to the lime-tree, who will give me leaves to give to the spring, who will give me water to give to Hickety, my dear hen, who is fighting for her life in the hazelwood."

"You'll get no wood till you bring me an axe," answered the
woodcutter.

And the cock ran off to the smith: "Dear smith, give me an axe to give to the woodcutter, who will give me wood to give to the bakeress, who will give me a bannock to give to the thresher, who will give me corn to give to the sow, who will give me bristles to give to the shoemaker, who will give me shoes to give to the Virgin Mary, who will give me ribbons of red gold to give to the lime-tree, who will give me leaves to give to the spring, who will give me water to give to Hickety, my dear hen, who is fighting for her life in the hazelwood."

"You'll get no axe till you bring me charcoal," answered the smith.

And the cock ran off to the charcoal burner: "Dear charcoal burner, give me charcoal to give to the smith, who will give me an axe to give to the woodcutter, who will give me wood to give to the bakeress, who will give me a bannock to give to the thresher, who will give me corn to give to the sow, who will give me bristles to give to the shoemaker, who will give me shoes to give to the Virgin Mary, who will give me ribbons of red gold to give to the lime-tree, who will give me leaves to give to the spring, who will give me water to give to Hickety, my dear hen, who is fighting for her life in the hazelwood."

And the charcoal burner felt sorry for the cock and gave him charcoal. And the smith got charcoal, and the woodcutter an axe, and the bakeress wood, and the thresher a bannock, and the sow corn, and the shoemaker bristles, and the Virgin Mary shoes, and the lime-tree ribbons of red gold, and the spring leaves, and the cock water that he gave to Hickety, his dear hen, who was fighting for her life in the hazelwood. And so she got well again.

EAST OF THE SUN
AND WEST
OF THE MOON

Once upon a time there was a poor cottar who had many children and little to give them in the way of food or clothing. They were bonny children all, but the fairest was the youngest daughter. She was as fair, as fair as could be.

One Thursday evening late in the autumn, it was dark and stormy, and the wind and the rain made the walls creak, and the family sat huddled round the hearth, each busy with his own task. All of a sudden, there came three knocks on the window-pane. The cottar went out to see who it was and outside the door he found a big, big white bear standing there.

"Good evening, cottar," said the white bear.

"Good evening," said the man.

"If you will give me your youngest daughter, I will make you as rich as you are now poor!" said the bear.

The cottar thought it very fine indeed that he was to be so rich, but he felt he ought to speak with his daughter first. And he went in and told her that there was a big white bear outside who promised to make them all very rich if only he could have her. She was unwilling, but the cottar went outside again and settled with the white bear that he should return on the following Thursday evening and receive an answer. In the meantime the family gave her no peace and kept on describing all the riches that would be theirs and all the good things that she would have herself. And at last she gave in. She washed and mended her tattered clothes and adorned herself as best she could. Soon she was ready to set out, for there was little enough she had to take with her.

On the following Thursday evening the white bear came to fetch her. She sat upon his back with her bundle, and then off they went.

After they had gone a long way, the white bear said, "Are you afraid?"

No, she wasn't, she said.

"Hold on to my fur, and you will be quite safe," he said.

She rode on much farther, and at long last they came to a tall mountain. There the white bear knocked, a gate opened, and they entered a palace with many rooms, well lit and gleaming with gold and silver. And they came into a great hall, where a table was laid ready, and you cannot imagine how rich and splendid it was. Then the white bear gave her a silver bell. And if there was anything she wanted, she had only to ring the bell and she would have it. When she had eaten and the evening drew on, she felt sleepy after her journey and thought she would like to go to bed. She rang the silver bell, and scarcely had she touched it when she found herself in a chamber where there stood a bed all ready as beautiful as you could wish to lie in, with silk covers and curtains and fringes of gold. And everything in the chamber was of gold and silver. After she had gone to bed and put out the light, someone came in and lay down beside her. This was the white bear, who cast off his bear-like shape at night. But she could never see him, for he always came after she had put out the light and by daybreak he had always disappeared.

For a while all went well, but then she took to sitting about still and sad. She was there alone all day and longed to be home with her parents and her brothers and sisters. At last the white bear asked her what was the matter, and she answered that it was so lonely there. She was all by herself and longed to be home with her family. It was because she could not visit them that she felt so sad. "I should be able to take you there," said the white bear. "But you must promise me not to speak to your mother alone. Speak to her only when the others are listening nearby. For she is sure to take you by the hand," he said, "and lead you into a chamber to talk with you alone. But you must never do it, otherwise you will make us both very unhappy."

One Sunday the white bear said that they could set off to see her parents. They started out and she sat upon his back. Their journey lasted a long, long time, and at last they came to a big white farm-house. There were her brothers and sisters running about playing, and it was all so lovely there that it was a joy to see. "That is where your parents live," said the white bear. "But don't forget what I have told you. Otherwise you will make me unhappy and yourself too." And she swore she would not forget, and when she reached the house the white bear turned back and was soon gone.

Her parents greeted her in all gladness. They scarcely knew how to express their thanks for all she had done for them. Now they were so well off, and they all asked her how she was getting on. She said she was very comfortable and had everything she could wish for. What else she told them it is hard to say, but I doubt whether they got very much out of her.

Then, in the afternoon, after they had eaten dinner, things happened just as the white bear had said. Her mother wished to speak to her alone. But she remembered what the white bear had told her, and refused. "What we have to speak of," she said, "we can speak of here as well as anywhere." But in some way or other her mother ended by persuading her, and she felt she had to tell her everything.

She told her how someone always came in and lay down beside her after she had put out the light at night, and she never saw him, because he had always disappeared by daybreak. And she was sad, for she wanted to see him so much, and during the day she was all by herself there, so deserted and lonely it was.

"Good gracious, you may well be sleeping with a troll," said her mother. "But let me show you a way to see him. I can give you a candle-end to hide in your bosom. Light it and look at him while he is asleep. But take care not to let the tallow drip on him."

And she took the candle and hid it in her bosom, and in the evening the white bear came and fetched her.

After they had travelled some way, the white bear asked her whether things had turned out as he said they would.

She had to confess that he was right.

"Well, if you have taken your mother's advice, you have made us both unhappy and all is over between us," he said.

28

But she said she had done no such thing.

When she reached home and went to bed, the same thing happened again. Someone came in and lay down beside her. But in the course of the night, when she was sure he was asleep, she got up and lit the candle. She let it shine on him and then she saw that he was the most beautiful prince you could wish to look upon. And she fell so deeply in love with him that she felt she must die if she did not kiss him at once. She kissed him, but as she did so she spilled three drops of hot tallow on his shirt and woke him.

"What have you done?" he cried. "Now you have made both of us unhappy. If only you had been patient for a year, I should have been saved and freed from the spell. For I have a stepmother who has bewitched me, so that I am a white bear by day and a human creature by night. But now all is over between us. Now I must leave you and go to her. She lives in a castle that lies east of the sun and west of the moon, and in that castle there is a princess with a nose two yards long. I shall have to wed her now."

She wept and moaned, but it was no use. He had to leave her. And she asked if she could go with him.

No, that was impossible.

"Tell me the way, then, so I can try to find you. Can't I do that?"

Yes, she could try to search for him. But there was no way there. The castle was east of the sun and west of the moon and she would never be able to find it.

In the morning when she awoke, both the prince and the palace were gone. She lay in a tiny glade in the middle of a dense, dark forest and beside her was the same bundle of rags she had left home with. After she had rubbed the sleep out of her eyes and cried to her heart's content, she set out on her way. She walked for many days, until she came to a high mountain.

There sat an old woman playing with a golden apple. She asked the old woman whether she knew the way to the prince who lived with his stepmother in a castle that lay east of the sun and west of the moon and who was to wed a princess with a nose two yards long.

"How do you come to know him?" asked the old woman "Are you the one who was going to wed him?"

Yes, she said, she was.

"Oh, you're the one!" said the woman. All I know about him is that he lives in the castle that lies east of the sun and west of the moon. And you'll be there late or you'll be there never, but you can borrow my horse and ride to my neighbour. Maybe she can tell you where it is. And when you get to her, just slap the horse under the left ear and order it to go home again. And you can take this golden apple with you."

She jumped up on the horse and rode a long, long way. At last she came to a mountain where there sat an old woman winding yarn on a golden reel. She asked the old woman whether she knew the way to the castle that lay east of the sun and west of the moon. And, like the first woman, she said that she knew

nothing about it except that it lay east of the sun and west of the moon. "And you'll be there late or you'll be there never, but you can borrow my horse and ride to my nearest neighbour. Maybe she will know. And when you get to her, just slap the horse under the left ear and order it to go home again," she said. And she gave her the golden reel, saying it was sure to come in handy.

The girl jumped up on the horse, and rode and rode again ever so far. And at long last she reached a high mountain where there sat an old woman turning a golden spindle. And she asked her whether she knew the way to the prince and where the castle was, that lay east of the sun and west of the moon.

And the same thing happened. "Maybe it was you who was going to wed that prince?" said the old woman.

Yes, that was so.

But she knew no more about the way than the other two. East of the sun and west of the moon she knew it was. "And you'll be there late or you'll be there never," she said. "But you can borrow my horse. I think you'd better ride to the East Wind and ask him. Maybe he knows of it and can blow you there. And when you get to him, you have only to slap the horse under the ear, and it will go home again." And she gave her the golden spindle. "It may come in handy," said the woman.

She rode a long way for many days before she got there. But at last she came to the East Wind and she asked him whether he could tell her the way to the prince who lived east of the sun and west of the moon.

Yes, the East Wind said he had heard of the prince and the castle too. But he did not know the way, for he had never blown as far as that. "But if you like, I can take you to my brother, the West Wind. Maybe he knows, for he is much stronger. You can sit upon my back, and I shall carry you there."

And she did so. And the wind blew strong. And when they got to the West Wind, they went in and the East Wind said that he had brought with him a girl who was to have wed the prince who lived in the castle that lay east of the sun and west of the moon. Now she was travelling in search of him, and he had carried her as far as this, and they wanted to inquire whether the West Wind knew where the castle was.

"No, I've never blown as far as that," said the West Wind. "But if you like, I can take you to the South Wind, for he is much stronger than either of us and he has roamed far and wide. Maybe he can tell you. You can sit on my back and I'll carry you there."

She did so. And they rushed along to the South Wind, and as far as I know it was a quick journey. When they arrived, the West Wind asked whether he could tell the girl the way to the castle that lay east of the sun and west of the moon, for it was she who was supposed to wed the prince.

"Indeed," said the South Wind. "Is she the one? Well, I've wandered about a bit in my time," he said, "but I've never blown as far as that. But if you like, I can take you to my brother, the North Wind. He is the eldest and strongest of us all. And if he doesn't know where it is, you'll never find out anywhere. You can sit on my back, and I'll carry you there."

She sat on his back and off he went like an arrow. And the journey was soon over.

When they approached the home of the North Wind, he was so wild and unruly that a cold gust of air came at them from far, far off.

"What do you-oo-oo want?" he whistled, far away, sending an icy chill through them.

"Oh, you needn't be so severe," said the South Wind. "It's only me, and this girl here who was supposed to wed the prince that lives in the castle that lies east of the sun and west of the moon. And now she wants to ask you whether you have been there and can tell her the way, since she is anxious to find him again.

"Yes, I-ee-ee know where it is," said the North Wind. "Once upon a time I blew an aspen leaf there, but I was so tired afterwards that I couldn't blow at all for days and days. But if you really want to get there, and if you aren't afraid of coming with me, I'll carry you on my back and see whether I can blow you as far as that."

She said that she wanted to go there and had to go there, if only there were a way of some kind, and she was not afraid of

what they risked.

"Well, you had better stay the night here," said the North Wind. "We are sure to need at least a day if we are to complete our journey."

Early next morning the North Wind woke her. And he gathered all his strength and made himself so mighty and strong that it was terrible to see. Then off they sped, high up in the air, as if they were aiming to strike the end of the world in a second. There was such a storm in the countryside that woods and houses were blown down. And when they passed over the ocean, hundreds of ships were wrecked. And they went on flying far, far away, so far you would not believe it, out over the ocean, until the North Wind grew so spent and weary that he could not blow any more. And they sank down lower and lower, and at last they flew so low that the tops of the waves were lapping round her heels.

"Are you afraid?" said the North Wind.

No, she said, she wasn't.

But they were not far from land now, and the North Wind had just enough strength left to drop her on the shore beneath the windows of the castle that lay east of the sun and west of the moon. And by then he was so tired and wretched that he had to rest for many a day before he could fly home again.

Next morning she sat down outside the castle windows and began playing with the golden apple. And the first person she saw was the nosey creature who was betrothed to the prince.

"What do you want for that golden apple of yours?" she said, opening the window.

"It's for sale for neither silver nor gold," said the girl.

"If it's not for sale for gold or for silver, what do you want for it? You can have whatever you like," said the princess.

"Well, if I could visit the prince who is here and spend this night with him, then I could let you have it," said she who had come with the North Wind.

And it was settled she could do so.

The princess got the golden apple. But when the girl came up to the prince's room that night, he was sound asleep. She called to him and shook him, and she wept and she cried out to him, but she could not get him to wake. In the morning, at break of day,

33

the princess with the long nose came and sent her away again.

During the day she sat outside the castle windows winding yarn on her golden reel. And the same thing happened. The princess asked her want she wanted for it, and she said that it was for sale for neither silver nor gold, but that, if she could have leave to spend the night with the prince, then the princess could have it. But when she came to join him, he was sound asleep again, and though she wept and shouted to him and shook him, he still slept on so deeply that she could not rouse him at all. And when day broke the next morning, the princess with the long nose came and sent her outside again.

Later in the day, the girl sat under the castle windows turning her golden spindle. And the princess with the long nose was eager to have that too. She opened her window and asked her what she wanted for it. The girl replied as she had done twice before, that it was for sale for neither silver nor gold, but that, if she could visit the prince who was there and spend the night with him, then the princess could have it. And she was allowed to do so. But it so happened that there were some Christian folk who were captives there and who were in the chamber next to where the prince was. They had heard a strange woman in his room crying and calling to him for two nights together and they said so to the prince. And that night, when the princess came with a hot drink for him, he pretended to drink it and poured it to one side, for now he realised it was a sleeping potion.

When the girl came in this time, the prince was awake. And he made her tell him how she had found the way there. "You've come just in time," said the prince. "The wedding-day is tomorrow. But I don't want to marry that nosey trollop, and you are the only one who can save me. I'm going to say that I want my bride to show me how skilled she is, and I'll ask her to wash the shirt with the three spots of tallow on it. She's sure to try, because she doesn't know that it was you who put them there. But this task can only be done by Christian folk and not by a pack of trolls like these. And I'm going to say that I'll have no bride but the one who can do this task, and then I'll ask you."

34   And great joy and delight was theirs that night. The day after,

when it was time for the wedding, the prince said, " First I'd like my bride to show me how skilled she is."

Of course, he could see her do anything at all, said the stepmother.

"I have a fine shirt that I wish to wear as my wedding shirt, but it has three spots of tallow on it and I'd like them washed off. And I have sworn that I shall take no bride but the one who has the skill to do this task. And if my bride cannot do it, then she is not worth having."

This sounded easy enough and they were willing to try. The long-nosed princess began washing as best she could. But the more she rubbed the stains, the larger they grew.

"Oh, you can't wash shirts," said the old troll, her mother. "Let me do it!" But she had scarcely touched the shirt when it grew much dirtier, and the more she washed and rubbed the stains, the larger and darker they became, and the shirt got worse and worse.

So the other trolls wanted to try to wash it, but the longer they kept at it, the dirtier and uglier it became, and in the end the whole shirt looked as if it had been dragged up the chimney.

"What a pack of good-for-nothings!" said the prince. "There is a beggar girl outside the window here. I'm sure she is much better at washing clothes than any of you. Come in here, my girl!" he shouted.

And in she came.

"Can you wash this shirt clean?" he said.

"Oh, I'm not sure," she said, "but I'll see if I can."

And no sooner had she touched the shirt and dipped it in water than it became as white as the driven snow and whiter still.

"You shall be my bride!" said the prince.

So then the old troll woman flew into such a rage that she burst. And the princess with the long nose and all the little trolls must have burst too, for I have heard nothing of them since. The prince and his bride set free all the good Christians who were captives there. And then they took all the gold and silver they could carry, and moved far away from the castle that lay east of the sun and west of the moon.

PER, PAUL
AND
ESPEN ASKELAD

There was once a man who had three sons, Per and Paul and Espen Askelad. But he was as poor as a church mouse, and his sons were all he had. So he told the three of them time and again that they would have to go out into the world to earn their bread, for if they stayed at home they had only a life of hunger before them.

Far away from the poor man's cottage the king had his farm. And right outside the king's windows an oak had sprung up and this oak was so mighty and tall that it shut out the light from the king's dwelling. The king had promised a great deal of money to whoever could cut down the oak. But no one could do it because, as soon as one piece was chopped off the trunk, two more grew there on the spot. And the king also wanted a well dug to supply water all the year round. Each of his neighbours owned a well, but he had none and he felt it was a disgrace. To anyone who could dig a well to provide water all the year the king had promised money and other riches, but no one could do it because the royal farm was high up on a hill, and whenever they started digging they struck hard rock a few inches down. Now the king had made up his mind that he wanted these tasks done. And he let it be proclaimed from the church doors all over the land that whoever could fell the great oak beside his dwelling and make him a well providing water all the year should be given his daughter in marriage and half his kingdom.

And I can assure you that there were many who were anxious to try their luck, but for all their hacking and chopping and all their burrowing and digging they got no farther. Every stroke made the oak thicker and thicker, and the rocky hillside showed no sign of getting any softer. The time came when the three brothers wished to set out and try their fortune too. Their father was well pleased, for he thought that even if they did not win the princess and half the kingdom they might find service in the household of a worthy man, and that was as much as he hoped for. And when the brothers made up their minds to go to the king's farm, their father gave his consent at once, and Per and Paul and Espen Askelad set off together.

After a while they came to a slope covered with spruce, and above it was a tall, steep hill. And far up they could hear a sound of chopping.

"I wonder what it is we can hear chopping on the hill up there?" said Espen Askelad.

"You're a marvel at wondering!" said Per and Paul. "Surprising, isn't it, to hear a woodcutter at work on the hill!"

"I think I'd like to see what it is," said Espen Askelad and off he went.

"If you're such a booby, it won't do you any harm to learn to walk as well!" his brothers shouted after him. But Espen did not bother about them. He climbed up the hillside and followed the sound of chopping, and at last he found it came from an axe that was busily cutting the trunk of a pine-tree.

"Good day," said Espen Askelad. "I see you're busy chopping."

"Yes, I've been here chopping a long, long time waiting for you," answered the axe.

"Well, here I am!" said Espen, and he took the axe and knocked off the handle and packed both axe and handle in his knapsack.

When he joined his brothers below, they teased and laughed at him. "What was the surprise up on the hill?" they said.

"Oh, it was only an axe we heard," said Espen.

Having walked on farther, they came to a rocky cliff where they could hear a sound of hammering and digging.

"I wonder what it is we can hear hammering and digging on the cliff up there?" said Espen Askelad.

"If you're such a marvel at wondering," said Per and Paul, "haven't you ever noticed woodpeckers hammering at trees before?"

"Yes, but I'd like to go and see what it is," said Espen. And the more they laughed and made fun of him, the less he cared. He climbed up to the cliff and when he got there he saw a pick hammering and digging.

"Good day," said Espen Askelad. "I see your're hammering and digging all alone."

"Yes," said the pick. "I've been here hammering and digging a long, long time waiting for you."

"Well, here I am!" said Espen once more, and he took the pick and knocked off the handle and put it in his knapsack. Then he walked down to join his brothers.

"You must have seen something wonderful on the cliff up there!" said Per and Paul.

"Nothing special. It was only a pick we heard," answered Espen.

They went on for a while until they came to a brook. By now they were all thirsty after their journey, and they lay down beside the brook to drink.

"Now I wonder just where this water comes from?" said Espen Askelad.

"Now I wonder whether you're quite right in your head?" said Per, and Paul too. "If you're not mad already, you'll be mad soon enough with all your wondering about this and that. Where does the brook come from? Haven't you ever seen water flowing from a spring in the ground?"

"Yes, but I'd still like to see where it comes from," said Espen. He started running upstream, and though his brothers shouted and laughed at him he took no notice and went on running.

Much farther up, the brook became smaller and smaller. And he kept on following it until at last he saw a big walnut out of which the water bubbled and flowed.

"Good day," said Espen once more. "I see you're bubbling and singing all alone."

"Oh, yes," said the walnut. "I've been here bubbling and singing a long, long time waiting for you."

"Well, here I am!" said Espen. He took a piece of moss and stuffed it in the hole so that the water could not run out, and he put the walnut in his knapsack and went down again to join his brothers.

"And now you've seen where the water comes from! It must have been a strange sight," said Per and Paul together.

"It was just running out of a hole," said Espen. And the other two laughed and made fun of him once more, but Espen did not let them worry him. "Still, I enjoyed seeing it," he said.

They walked on and they came to the king's farm. But since everyone in the kingdom had heard that they could win the princess and half the kingdom if they cut down the great oak and dug a well for the king, so many had come to try their luck that the oak was twice as huge as it had been to begin with, for you
will remember that two new pieces grew for every one that was

chopped off. And so the king had now decreed that all those who tried and could not fell the oak should be banished to an island and have their ears cropped.

But the two elder brothers were not afraid of what lay in store, for they were quite sure they could cut down the oak. The eldest brother Per was the first to try his luck. But he fared the same as all the others who had chopped the oak. For every piece he cut off, two new ones grew instead, and the king's men seized him and cropped his ears and set him out on the island. Then Paul wanted his turn, and his lot was the same. After he had hacked two or three times and everyone saw the oak growing thicker, the king's men took him and put him on the island and cropped his ears even closer, because they thought he ought to have learnt his lesson.

Then Espen Askelad wanted to try.

"If you are so eager to look like a marked sheep, we can crop your ears at once and spare you further trouble!" said the king, who was angry at the thought of the elder brothers.

"I'd rather like to have a try first," said Espen, and they had to let him.

He brought out his axe from his knapsack and fixed on its handle again. "Hew and cut!" said Espen to the axe. And it chopped and chopped so the splinters flew and it was not long before the oak was on the ground. After this Espen took his pick and fastened on the handle. "Dig and delve!" said Espen. And the pick hammered and dug and threw up earth and stones, and there was no stopping the sinking of the well this time. When it was deep and broad enough, Espen Askelad took out his walnut, set it in a corner at the bottom, and pulled out the moss. "Bubble and flow!" said Espen, and the water came spouting forth from the hole in the nut and in no time the well was full to the brim.

And so Espen felled the oak that shut out the light from the king's windows and he made a well for the king's farm, and he won the princess and half the kingdom, as the king had promised. But it was just as well for Per and for Paul that they lost their ears, otherwise they would have heard everyone saying over and over again that Espen Askelad had not wondered in vain.

40

THE BOY
AND THE DEVIL

Once there was a boy walking along a road cracking nuts. He came upon one that was worm-eaten, and just then he met the devil.

"Is it true what they say," said the boy, "that the devil can make himself as small as he will and force his way through a pin-prick?"

"Yes," answered the devil.

"Let me see you creep into this nut, then," said the boy. And the devil did so.

When he had crept right in through the worm-hole, the boy pushed a twig into it. "Now I've got you," he said, and put the nut in his pocket.

Further along the road he came to a forge. There he went in and asked the smith if he would crack open the nut for him.

"Yes, that's easy enough," replied the smith. And he took his smallest hammer, placed the nut on the anvil and hit it, but it would not break. So he took a bigger hammer, but that was not heavy enough either. And he tried an even bigger one, and that was no good. Then the smith got angry, and seized his sledge-hammer. "I'll smash you if it's the last thing I do!" said he and struck with all his might. And then the nut burst into splinters with such a roaring crash that half the roof flew off and it seemed as if the whole smithy would tumble down.

"The flaming devil must have been in that nut!" said the smith.

"He was!" said the boy.

THE TWO
STEPSISTERS

Once upon a time there was a couple who married and each of them already had a daughter. The elder daughter, the wife's child, was lazy and idle and would never do a single thing. The younger daughter, the husband's child, was clever and willing to work, yet she could never manage to please her stepmother and both her stepmother and her elder sister wished to be rid of her. One day the two sisters were told to spin beside the well. The elder sister was to spin flax, but the younger sister was given nothing but bristles. "I know you're always so quick and smart," said the elder sister. "All the same I'm not afraid of trying a spinning match with you." And it was agreed that the first one to break her thread was to be put in the well. It was not long before the younger sister's thread broke, and she had to be thrown down the well. But when she fell to the bottom she did not hurt herself, and around her on all sides she saw a beautiful green meadow.

She walked through the meadow and came to a brush fence which she thought she would climb over. "Oh, don't tread on me too hard," said the brush fence. "And then I shall help you some time." And she made herself as light as a feather and trod with such care that she scarcely touched it at all.

And she went on farther until she came to a brindle cow with a milk-pail hanging on its horns. It was a big, pretty cow and its udders were full and swollen. "Oh, please milk me," said the cow. "I'm bursting with milk. Drink as much as you like and pour the rest over my hoofs, and some time I shall help you in return."

The girl did as the cow asked. She had hardly touched its teats when the milk spurted into the pail. She drank and quenched her thirst and the rest she poured over the cow's hoofs. And she put the pail back on its horns.

After she had walked on again through the meadow, she met a huge ram that had long, thick wool trailing after it, and on one of its horns there hung a pair of shears. "Oh, do clip my wool," said the ram. "I'm dragging along all this heavy wool, and I'm so hot I'm near to stifling. Take as much as you like, and wind the rest round my neck, and I shall help you some time later." She was ready to help at once, and the ram climbed up on her lap. And it lay so still and she sheared it so neatly that its skin did not receive the slightest scratch. Then she took all she wanted of the wool and wound the rest round the ram's neck.

A little farther on she came to an apple-tree so loaded with apples that all its boughs were bent to the ground, and by the trunk was a little staff. "Oh, please pick my apples," said the tree, "so my boughs can be straight again, for it hurts me to stand so crooked. But do treat me gently and take care not to spoil my branches. Eat as many apples as you like and place the rest by my root, and I shall help you in return." She picked those she could reach and she took the staff and shook down the other apples carefully. Then she ate her fill and stored the rest neatly at the foot of the tree.

She went on a long, long way until she reached a large farm where there lived a witch and her daughter. There she went in and asked for service. "Oh, it's no use you coming here," said the witch. "We've had a lot of servants, but none of them have been any good." Still, she kept asking politely to be taken on and in the end they let her be their servant. And the witch gave her a sieve and told her to fetch water in it. She thought it foolish to fetch water in a sieve; all the same, she went out. And when she came to the well, the little birds sang:

> "Press in clay
> And straw there lay!
> Press in clay
> And straw there lay!"

She did so, and she could carry water in the sieve well enough. But when she got home with the water, the witch looked at the sieve and said, "This is some hanky-panky trick."

The witch told her next to go to the cow-stable and clear away the manure and do the milking. But when she got there, she found a shovel so big and heavy that she could not lift it at all, let alone work with it. And now she had no idea what to do. But the little birds sang to her to take the broom and sweep out a little, and all the rest of the manure would follow after. She did so, and she had scarcely set to work with the broom when the whole stable was as clean as if had been cleared and swept all over. After that she began milking the cows, but they were so restless that they kicked and stamped and she could get no milk from them at all. And then the birds outside sang:

"A tiny jet,
A drop so small,
Send to the songsters,
Send to them all!"

And she did so. She sprayed a tiny jet of milk out to the little birds. And all the cows stood still and let her milk them and neither stamped nor kicked. Not one of them stirred an inch.

When the witch saw her come in with the milk, she said, "This is some hanky-panky trick. But now you can take this black wool and wash it white." The girl had no idea how to manage this, for she had never seen anyone succeed in washing black wool white, though she said nothing. She took the wool and carried it to the well. Then the little birds sang to her to dip the wool in the large tub standing there and she would soon get it white.

"Well," said the witch, when she came back with the wool, "it's no use keeping you here. You can do everything and you'll end by worrying the life out of me. It's best for you to be off."

And so the witch placed three caskets before her, one red, one green, and one blue. Of these she could choose any one as payment for her service. She did not know which to choose, but the little birds sang:

"Let the green one be,
Let the red one be,

Take the blue one, the blue one
With crosses three."

And she chose the blue one, as the little birds told her in their song. "Curse you!" cried the witch. "You'll pay for this."

Just as the younger sister was leaving the farm-house, the witch hurled a bolt of red-hot iron at her. And at once she darted behind the door and hid so that it missed her, because the little birds had told her beforehand what to do. She set off as fast as she could, but when she got as far as the apple-tree, she heard a rumbling sound on the road behind her. That was the witch and her daughter who were after her. And the girl was so afraid she did not know which way to turn.

"Come over here," said the apple-tree. "And I shall help you. Come and hide among my branches, because if they get hold of you they will take your casket away and tear you to pieces."

She hid there and the next thing she knew was that the witch and her daughter had caught up with her.

"Have you seen a girl pass this way?" asked the witch.

"Oh, yes," answered the apple-tree. "A girl ran past here a while ago, but by now she must be so far away that you cannot reach her."

And the witch turned back and went home again.

The girl continued on her way, but when she got as far as the ram, she heard such a dreadful rumbling that she did not know what to do, she was so frightened. She knew it was the witch, who had changed her mind and run after her again.

"Come over here. I can help you," said the ram. "Hide under my wool so they cannot see you. Otherwise they will take away your casket and tear you to pieces."

And the next moment, the witch came hurrying along.

"Have you seen a girl pass by here?" she asked the ram.

"Oh, yes," said the ram. "I saw a girl a while ago, but she was running so fast that you will not catch up with her."

And the witch turned back and went home.

When the girl had got to where the cow was, she heard a loud rumbling along the road once more.

"Come over here," said the cow. "And I shall help you. Hide under my udders. Otherwise the witch will come and take away your casket and tear you to pieces."

She was not long in coming. "Have you seen a girl pass by here?" said the witch to the cow.

"Yes, I did see a girl a little while ago. But she is far away now, she was running so quickly. I don't think you can catch up with her," said the cow. And the witch turned back and went home again.

After the girl had gone on a long, long way and she was not far from the brush fence, she heard such a rumble behind her on the road that she grew full of fear, because she guessed that it was the witch who had started following her again.

"Come over here and let me help you," said the brush fence. "Creep under my twigs so they cannot see you. Otherwise they will take away your casket and tear you to pieces." And she hid quickly under the twigs of the fence.

"Have you seen a girl around here?" said the witch to the brush fence.

"No, I haven't seen any girl," answered the brush fence. And it was so angry that it rustled and crackled. And it made itself so tall that there was no hope of anyone climbing over it. And all the witch could do was to turn back and go home.

When the younger sister came home safe and sound, the stepmother and her daughter were more envious of her than they had ever been. She was now much prettier and looked so lovely that it was a joy to see her. She was not allowed to be in the house, but was turned out and sent to the pigsty, which was to be her home. Here she washed everything clean and neat and then opened her casket to see what she had been given in payment for her service. And as she lifted the lid there appeared so much gold and silver and so many precious things that the walls and ceiling were all hung with them at once and the pigsty was grander than the finest royal dwelling. When the stepmother and her daughter saw all this, they were quite beside themselves and set to questioning her about the sort of work she had had. "Oh," she said, "you can guess what it was like from my wages. The household and the mistress I served were such that you have never seen the like."

And there and then the elder sister was eager to be off and work as a servant so that she could earn a casket of gold too. And they sat down to spin again. But this time the elder sister was to spin bristles and the younger sister flax, and whoever broke her thread first was to be put in the well. And soon enough the elder sister broke her thread, as you can imagine, and then she was thrown down the well.

And the same thing happened to her. She fell to the bottom but did not get hurt, and she found herself in a beautiful green meadow. After she had walked a while, she came to the brush fence.

"Don't tread on me too hard, and I shall help you in return," said the brush fence.

"Oh, a fine lot I care about a bundle of twigs," she said, and trampled on the fence so heavily that it snapped and cracked.

In a little while she came to the cow that was bursting with milk.

"Please milk me," said the cow. "And I shall help you later. Drink as much as you like, and pour the rest over my hoofs."

She did so. She milked the cow and then drank and drank. But there was none left to pour over the hoofs. And the pail she threw down on the ground and left there.

After she had gone on farther, she met the ram trailing his long wool after him.

"Oh, please clip my wool, and I shall do you a good turn later," said the ram. "Take as much of the wool as you like, and wind the rest round my neck."

And she did so, but she worked so clumsily that she cut big pieces off the ram, and she took all the wool with her.

Soon after, she reached the apple-tree that was now bowed down with fruit again.

"Please pick my apples so my boughs can be straight, for it hurts me so to be crooked," said the apple-tree. "But take care to treat me gently and not ruin my branches. Eat much as you like, and 48   place the rest neatly by my root, and I shall help you in return."

She picked the nearest fruit and she took the staff and knocked down those she could not reach. But she was as careless as could be, and beat and tore down large branches. She kept on eating all she could and scattered the rest under the tree.

After she had walked a while longer, she came to the farm where the witch lived. There she asked for service. The witch said that she did not want any servant girl, because either they were good-for-nothings or they were so sharp that they got hold of all she possessed. The elder sister would not give in, but insisted on entering her service. And the witch agreed to take her on as long as she proved herself useful.

The first thing she had to do was to fetch water in the sieve. She went to the well and poured water into the sieve, though as fast as she poured it in it ran out again. And the birds sang:

"Press in clay
And straw there lay!
Press in clay
And straw there lay!"

But she did not bother about the birds' song. She threw clay at the birds and frightened them all away. And she had to go home again with an empty sieve and was scolded by the witch.

She was told next to clear manure from the cow-stable and milk the cows. She thought such work beneath her. All the same she went into the stable, but when she got there she could not handle the shovel because it was so big. The birds told her, as they had told the younger sister, to take the broom and sweep out a little manure and then all the rest would follow. But she seized the broom and threw it at the birds. When she started the milking, the cows were so restless that they stamped and kicked, and each time she got a little milk in the pail, they upset it. The birds sang:

"A tiny jet,
A drop so small,
Send to the songsters,
Send to them all!"

But she struck and beat the cows and she threw all she could find at the little birds and made such a scene. And no manure did she clear and no milk did she get from the cows. And when she came home she was smacked and scolded by the witch. After that she had to wash the black wool white, but she was no better at that either.

The witch thought this bad enough, and she placed before her three caskets, one red, one green, and one blue. She told her that she had no use for her because she was a good-for-nothing, but that in payment for her service she could choose whichever casket she liked. And then the birds sang:

"Let the green one be,
Let the red one be,
Take the blue one, the blue one
With crosses three."

She took no heed of the birds' song, but chose the red one, which was brightest. And so she set out for home. And she had a peaceful journey, for no one came hurrying after her. When she reached home, her mother was as glad as could be, and they went straight into the parlour and placed the casket there. They believed that it was full of gold and silver and they thought that the walls and the ceiling would soon be gilded all over. But the moment they opened the casket, there poured forth nothing but serpents and toads. And whenever the elder sister opened her mouth, the same thing happened. There poured out serpents and toads and all kinds of vermin, so that at last no one could be in the same house with her. And these were the wages she received for serving in the house of the witch.

THE CAT
OF DOVRE

There was once a man up in Finnmark who caught a big white bear and he set out to take it to the King of Denmark. And it so happened that he came to the mountains of Dovre on Christmas Eve, and he went into a cottage where there lived a man by the name of Halvor. Here he asked for a night's shelter for himself and his white bear.

"Heaven help us all!" said the cottager. "We can give no shelter to strangers tonight, for every Christmas Eve there come so many trolls here that we all have to move out of the house and we have no roof over our own heads."

"Oh, I think you can still put me up," said the man. "My bear can sleep under the stove here, and the closet will do for me."

In the end, he was allowed to stay. Then the family moved out, having prepared a table laden with cream porridge and lye fish and sausages and all the good things that belong to a festive board.

All of a sudden, the trolls came in. Some were big and some were small, some had long tails and some had no tails, and some had long, long noses. And they ate and they drank and they tasted all the dishes.

But one of the little trolls caught sight of the white bear asleep under the stove. And he seized a piece of sausage, roasted it hot on the end of a fork, and toddled along and thrust it under the nose of the white bear, crying, "Pussy want a sausage?" And then the white bear started up with a mighty growl and chased the whole pack of them helter-skelter out of the house.

One year later Halvor was in the forest on the afternoon of Christmas Eve cutting wood for the Christmas season, for he was expecting the trolls again.

While he was busily chopping, he heard a voice call from the forest, "Halvor! Halvor!"

"Yes," said Halvor.

"Have you still got that big cat of yours?"

"Yes, she's at home asleep under the stove," said Halvor. "And now she has a litter of seven kittens who are all much bigger and angrier than she is!"

"Well, we won't be coming to visit you any more!" shouted the troll from the depths of the forest. And since that time the trolls have never eaten Christmas dinner at Halvor's cottage in Dovre.

THE SEVEN FOALS

Once upon a time there was a poor couple who lived in a miserable cottage in the depths of the forest and who barely managed to get enough to eat. But they had three sons, and the youngest was called Askelad, for he did nothing but sit by the fire poking and fiddling with the ashes.

One day the eldest son said that he wished to go out to service. His parents gave him leave to go, and he wandered out into the world. He walked and walked all day and towards evening he came to the farm of a king. There stood the king on the steps of his porch and asked him where he was going.

"Oh, I'm looking for service, master," said the lad.

"Will you serve in my household and keep watch over my seven foals?" asked the king. "If you can watch them a whole day and tell me in the evening what they eat and drink, I'll give you my daughter and half my kingdom. But if you fail, I'll cut three red strips off your back."

The lad thought this work sounded easy enough and agreed to do it.

Early next morning as dawn was breaking the groom let loose the seven foals. Off they bounded with the lad at their heels. And you can be sure they sped far, over hill and dale and through wood and mire. After the lad had been racing along behind them for some time, he began to feel tired, and, though he kept up the pace a while longer, he had soon had enough and was ready to give up the task. Then he came to a cleft rock where an old woman sat spinning on a distaff. When she caught sight of the lad sweating and running after the foals, she called out, "Come, my fair son, come here and let me louse you!" And the lad was more than willing. He settled down with the woman under the rock and put his head in her lap. And she loused him all day long while he lay idling there.

When evening approached, the lad wanted to be off. "I might as well stroll home again," he said, "because it's not much use going back to the king's farm."

"Wait till it gets a little darker," said the woman. "Then the king's foals will pass by here again and you can run back with them. Nobody knows that you have been lying here all day instead of watching the foals."

When they arrived, she gave the lad a flask of water and a clump of moss.. These he was to show to the king, and he was to say that these were the food and drink of the seven foals.

"Have you kept faithful watch all day, my lad?" said the king, when the lad came before him in the evening.

"Of course I have," said the lad.

"Can you tell me then what my seven foals eat and drink?" asked the king.

And the lad showed him the flask of water and the clump of moss that the woman had given him. "Here you see their food and there you see their drink," said the lad.

But the king understood well enough how faithfully he had watched and he was so angry that he gave orders for the lad to be turned out and sent home on the spot, and first he was to have three red strips cut off his back and salt rubbed on the wounds.

When the lad returned home, you can imagine how high his spirits were. He had gone out to service once, he said, but he would never do so again.

The next day, the second son said that he wished to go out into the world and try his fortune. His parents refused to let him go and told him to take a look at his brother's back. But the lad kept on insisting until in the end he was allowed to set out. After walking all day, he too came to the king's farm. There stood the king on the steps of his porch and asked him where he was going. And when the lad answered that he was looking for service, the king said that he could serve him and watch his seven foals. And the king fixed the same punishment and the same reward for him as he had done for his brother.

54   The lad agreed at once and entered the king's service, for he

felt sure he could mind the foals and tell the king what they ate and drank.

Early next morning at break of day the groom let loose the seven foals. Once more they sped over hill and dale, with the lad at their heels. But he did the same as his brother had done before him. After he had raced behind the foals a long, long time, tired and bathed in sweat, he passed a cleft rock where an old woman sat spinning on a distaff. And she called out to the lad, "Come, my fair son, come here and let me louse you!" And the lad was willing. The foals he left to run off on their own and he settled down with the woman under the rock. He sat there, and then he lay there, and idled away the day.

When the foals came back towards evening, he was also given a clump of moss and a flask of water to present to the king. But when the king asked the lad, "Can you tell me now what my seven foals eat and drink?" and the lad showed him the clump of moss and the flask of water and said, "Here you see their food and there you see their drink," the king got angry again. He gave orders that three red strips should be cut off his back and salt rubbed on the wounds and that he should be turned out and sent home on the spot. And after the lad returned home, he too told them all how he had fared. He said that he had gone out to service once and that he would never do so again.

On the third day, Askelad wished to be off. He wanted to try the task of watching the seven foals too, he said.

The other brothers laughed and jeered at him: "A fine job you'll make of it! We know what your chances are, after what's happened to us! You've never done a thing except squat there, poking the fire and fiddling with the ashes."

"Oh, I think I'll set off just the same," said Askelad. "I've made up my mind now." And although the others laughed and his parents implored him to stay, it made no difference. Askelad started on his way.

After he had walked all day, he too came to the king's farm at twilight. There stood the king on the steps of his porch and asked him where he was going.

"I'm looking for service," said Askelad.

"Where do you come from?" asked the king, for now he wanted to know more about those who entered his service.

Askelad explained where he came from and said he was the brother of the two who had been set to watch the king's seven foals. And then he asked if he could try his luck at watching them next day.

"Those rascals!" said the king, who grew angry each time he was reminded of them. "If you are a brother of those two, you must be a good-for-nothing. I've had enough of your sort!"

"Yes, but seeing I've come all the way here, couldn't you let me have a try too?" said Askelad.

"Well, if you're so keen to have your back flayed, it's all the same to me," said the king.

"I think I'd rather have the princess," said Askelad.

In the morning at daybreak the groom let loose the seven foals once more, and they sped over hill and dale and through wood and mire with Askelad at their heels.

After he had been running along behind them for some time, he too came to the cleft rock. There sat the old woman again spinning on her distaff and she called out to Askelad, "Come, my fair son, come here and let me louse you!" she said.

"Kiss my arse!" shouted Askelad, as he leapt and bounded along, holding on to a foal's tail.

When they had left the rock behind them, the youngest foal said to him, "Jump up and sit on my back. We have a long way to go yet." And he did so.

Then they went on much, much farther. "Can you see anything?" said the foal.

"No," said Askelad.

And then they went on again.

"Can you see anything?" asked the foal.

"Oh, no," said the lad.

When they had gone on even farther, the foal asked again, "Can you see anything now?"

"Yes, now I think I can see something white," said Askelad. "It looks like a great birch stump."

"We're going in there," said the foal.

When they came to the birch stump, the eldest foal took it and wrenched it to one side. And there was a door where the birch stump had stood. Beyond the door was a small room, and in the room there was barely more than a small hearth and a few stools. But behind the door hung a large, rusty sword and a small pitcher.

"Can you swing the sword?" asked the foal.

Askelad tried, but he could not do so. Then he had to drink from the pitcher, first once, then a second time, then a third time, and then he could wield it easily.

"Now you must take the sword with you," said the foal. "And with it you are to cut off the heads of all seven of us on your wedding-day. And so we shall become princes again, as we were before. For we are the brothers of the princess you are to wed when you can tell the king what we eat and drink. A wicked troll has cast a spell on us and changed us into beasts. After you have cut off our heads, you must take care to place each head by the tail of the body on which it was before. Then the spell will have no more power over us."

Askelad promised to do so, and they continued their journey.

When they had gone a long, long way, the foal asked, "Can you see anything?"

"No," said Askelad.

And they kept on going yet a while. "And now?" asked the foal. "Can you see anything?"

"Oh, no," said Askelad.

Then they sped along for many, many leagues, both up hill and down dale.

"Now?" said the foal. "Can't you see anything now?"

"Oh, yes," said Askelad. "I think I can see a strip of blue, far, far away."

"Yes, that's a river," said the foal. "We're going to cross it."

Over the river there was a fine, long bridge, and after they came to the other side, they went on much, much farther. Then the foal asked Askelad once more whether he could see anything.

Yes, this time he could see something dark in the distance, like a church tower.

"We're going in there too," said the foal.

When the foals entered the churchyard, they changed into human creatures and appeared as princes, in the richest garments you ever saw. And then they went into the church and received bread and wine from the priest who stood at the altar. Askelad went in with them. After the priest had laid his hands on the princes and blessed them, they went out of the church and Askelad followed them. And he carried away a flask of wine and a piece of altar-bread. As soon as the seven princes entered the churchyard, they changed into foals again. Then Askelad jumped up and sat on the back of the youngest one, and they went back the same way they had come, but much, much faster. They sped along first over the bridge, then past the birch stump, and then past the woman spinning under the rock. And they went so quickly that Askelad could not hear what the woman shouted after him, but he heard enough to grasp that she was in a furious rage.

It was nearly dark when they returned to the king's farm in the evening, and the king himself was standing in the yard waiting for them.

"Have you kept faithful watch all day?" said the king to Askelad.

58   "I've done my best," replied Askelad.

"Can you tell me then what my seven foals eat and drink?" asked the king.

Askelad brought out the altar-bread and the flask of wine and showed them to the king. "Here you see their food and there you see their drink," he said.

"Yes, you have kept faithful watch," said the king. "And you shall have the princess and half my kingdom."

And the king gave orders to prepare for a wedding that was to be the grandest ever heard of in the land. But while they were sitting at the wedding feast, the bridegroom rose and went out to the stable, saying that he had to fetch something he had forgotten there. Having entered the stable, he did as the foals had asked. He cut off the heads of all seven of them, beginning with the eldest and in proper order down to the youngest. And he took special care to place each head by the tail of the foal to which it belonged. And as he did so, they became princes again. When he came in to the wedding feast with the seven princes, the king was so happy that he kissed and embraced Askelad warmly, and his bride loved him even more than she had done before. "You already have half my kingdom," said the king. "And you will get the other half after my death, for my sons can acquire lands and kingdoms of their own, now that they have become princes again." And I can assure you that there was joy and merriment at that wedding.

I was there myself. But no one had any time to think of me. All I got to eat was a buttered oatcake, and that I left on the stove. And the cake burnt away, and the butter melted away, and not a crumb remained for me to swallow.

AASE
THE GOOSE-GIRL

Once there was a king who had so many geese that he had
to keep a gooseherd, called Aase. And she was known as Aase
the goose-girl.

It so happened that the Prince of England was out to seek a
wife, and he found Aase sitting in his way.

"Good day, little Aase. What are you doing there?" said the
prince.

"Oh, I'm patching and mending my clothes because I'm
expecting the Prince of England today," said Aase.

"You can't hope to wed him," said the prince.

"Oh, if I'm meant to have him, I'll wed him sure enough,"
said Aase.

Then artists were sent to all the kingdoms of the earth to
make portraits of the fairest princesses so that the prince might
choose among them. One of them pleased him so much that
he set out to make her his wife, and he was full of joy when
she became his sweetheart. But the prince had with him a magic
stone that he placed by his bed and this stone knew everything.
And when the princess came, Aase the goose-girl told her that
if she had had a sweetheart before or if she was troubled by
anything she did not want the prince to know then she had to
take care not to step over the magic stone by his bed, "for it
will tell him everything about you," she said. When the princess
heard this, she grew very disheartened. But then she hit upon
the idea of asking Aase to go up instead of her and sleep with
the prince that night, and, after he fell asleep, to change places
with her so that he could have his loved one beside him when
daylight came.

And they did so.

When Aase the goose-girl came in and trod on the stone, the prince asked, "Who is stepping into my bed?"

"A maiden pure and true!" said the stone, and they lay down to sleep. But later that night, the princess came and took Aase's place.

In the morning when it was time to get up, the prince asked the stone once more, "Who is stepping out of my bed?"

"One who has had three sweethearts," said the stone.

On hearing this, the prince would not have her, as you may well imagine. He sent her home again and took another sweetheart instead.

When he set out to visit her, he found Aase the goose-girl sitting in his way again.

"Good day, little Aase. What are you doing there?" said the prince.

"Oh, I'm patching and mending my clothes because I'm expecting the Prince of England today," said Aase.

"You can't hope to wed him," said the prince.

"Oh, if I'm meant to have him, I'll wed him sure enough," replied Aase.

And the same thing happened to the second princess as to the first, except that when she got up in the morning the magic stone said that she had had six sweethearts. The prince would not have her either and sent her away. But he thought he would try just once more to see whether he could find a maiden pure and true. He sought far and wide in many a land until he found a princess he liked.

But when he set out to visit her, he found Aase the goose-girl sitting in his way again.

"Good day, little Aase. What are you doing there?" said the prince.

"Oh, I'm patching and mending my clothes because I'm expecting the Prince of England today," said Aase.

"You can't hope to wed him," said the prince.

"Oh yes, if I'm meant to have him, I'll wed him sure enough," said Aase.

When the third princess came, Aase the goose-girl told her exactly what she had told the first two, that if she had had a sweetheart or if there was anything else she did not want the prince to know then she had to take care not to tread on the magic stone that the prince had by his bed, "because it tells him everything," she said. The princess was dejected when she heard this, but she was just as cunning as the other two and asked Aase to go up instead of her and sleep with the prince that night, and, after he fell asleep, to change places with her so that he could have his loved one beside him when daylight came.

And they did so.

When Aase the goose-girl came in and trod on the stone, the prince asked, "Who is stepping into my bed?"

"A maiden pure and true!" said the stone, and they lay down together.

During the night the prince placed a ring on Aase's finger,

and it was so tight that she could not get it off, for the prince guessed that something was wrong and he wanted to have a token by which he could recognise his true love. After the prince had fallen asleep, the princess came in and sent Aase down to the goose-pen and took her place.

In the morning when it was time to get up, the prince asked, "Who is stepping out of my bed?"

"One who has had nine sweethearts," said the stone. And on hearing this, the prince became so angry that he turned the princess out on the spot, and he asked the magic stone to explain the mystery of these princesses who had been stepping in and out; it was all quite beyond him, he said. The stone then told him the tale of how the three princesses had deceived him and sent Aase the goose-girl in their stead. But the prince wanted to find out for himself. So he went down to where Aase sat watching her geese to see whether she had the ring, because, he thought, if she did he had better make her his queen. When he met her, he noticed at once that she had tied a strip of cloth round one of her fingers, and he asked her why she had done so. "Oh, I've cut my finger so badly," said Aase the goose-girl. He insisted on seeing her finger, but Aase would not remove the cloth. The prince seized her finger, Aase tried to draw it back, and the cloth came off and he recognised his ring. Then he took her to the royal dwelling and gave her rich garments and fine jewels. And afterwards they were married. And so it happened that Aase the goose-girl wed the Prince of England after all, because she was meant to have him.

THE BOY WHO BECAME
A LION, A FALCON
AND AN ANT

Once upon a time there was a man who had only one son and who lived in wretched poverty. Before he breathed his last, he called his son to him and told him that all he had to leave him was a sword, a piece of sackcloth, and a handful of bread-crumbs. After his death, the young lad wished to set out and seek his fortune in the wide world. So he belted on the sword and he packed the breadcrumbs in the sackcloth for food, as his home was in a lonely place far up on a wooded hillside. His way lay across a mountain, and when he had climbed high enough to get a view of the moorland beyond, he saw a lion, a falcon, and an ant quarrelling over a dead horse. The boy grew pale at the sight of the lion. But it called to him to come and settle their quarrel and share out the horse so that each might get his due.

The boy took his sword and divided the horse as best he could. The lion he gave the large joints. The falcon he gave the liver and lights and other tidbits. And the ant got the head. And having done so, he said, "Now I think each has his fair share. The lion should get the most, for he is biggest and strongest. The falcon should get the best, for he is such a dainty feeder. And the ant should get the skull, for he likes creeping in nooks and corners."

They were all very pleased to have the horse shared out in this way, and they asked him what he wanted for making such a just settlement. "If I have been of service to you and you are satisfied, I am happy enough," he said, "and I want no payment." But they all said he deserved something. "If there is nothing else you want," said the lion, "you can have three wishes." But the boy did not know what to wish for. Then the lion asked him if he would like to wish he could turn into a

lion, and the other two asked him if he would like to be able to turn into a falcon and an ant. The boy thought this would be useful and he made the three wishes.

He threw aside his sword and sackcloth, changed into a falcon, and began to fly. He kept on flying till he was above a great lake. But far out over the lake he started to feel so tired and his wings were so sore that he could fly no longer, and then he caught sight of a rocky crag rising out of the water. There he stopped and rested. It was a strange-looking crag, and he spent a while exploring it.

After he had rested, he turned into a little falcon again and flew on until he reached the king's farm. There he settled on a tree outside the windows where the princess lived. As soon as she saw the bird, she wanted to catch it. She coaxed it to come to her and once the falcon was in her chamber she was all ready to slam the window shut and in a twinkling she had the bird in a cage.

5

When night came, the boy changed into an ant and crept out of the cage. And then he became a boy again and went and sat with the princess. And she got such a fright that she screamed and woke the king who came in to ask what was the matter.

"There's someone here!" cried the princess. And by that time the boy had become an ant, crept into the cage, and turned into a falcon again. The king could not find any cause for alarm. And so he told his daughter that she must have been troubled by a nightmare. But no sooner had the king left the room than the boy did the same again. He crept out of the cage as an ant, became himself once more, and sat beside the princess.

She gave a loud scream, and the king came in again to see what was the matter.

"There is someone here!" cried the princess. But the boy darted into the cage once more and sat there as a falcon. The king looked about and hunted high and low, and when he found nothing he grew angry at having his night's rest disturbed, and he told his daughter she was talking nonsense. "If you scream again," he said, "I'll make you realise you've got a king for a father."

But scarcely had the king closed the door behind him when the boy was beside the princess again. This time she did not scream, though she was so afraid that she did not know which way to turn.

And the boy asked her why she was so frightened.

She told him that she was promised to a big troll, and on the very first day she walked in the open air the troll was to come and carry her off. And when the boy had appeared in her chamber, she thought it was the big troll. Every Thursday morning the troll sent an envoy, and that envoy was a dragon to whom the king had to yield nine fat swine each time it came. And therefore he had proclaimed that whoever could free him from the dragon should be given the princess in marriage and half the kingdom.

The boy said he would do this, and next morning the princess went to the king and told him there was someone there who was willing to free him from the dragon and the tribute

of swine. The king was pleased to hear this, for the dragon had eaten up so many swine that there were scarcely any left in all the kingdom. It happened to be a Thursday that day, and so the boy went to where the dragon came each week to receive the swine. One of the tillers from the king's farm showed him the way.

Soon enough the dragon came along. It had nine heads and it was so full of fury when there was no sign of its meal of pork that it spat out fiery flames and charged at the boy as if it would swallow him alive. But in a twinkling the boy became a lion, and he fought with the dragon and tore off one head after the other. The dragon was strong too, and it spouted blazing venom. But at length it had only one head left and that was the mightiest. The boy kept on fighting until he tore the last head off as well, and that was the end of the dragon. Then he went to the king with the news, and there was rejoicing in the household and the princess was to be his bride.

But one day when they were walking in the garden, the big troll suddenly came upon them and seized the princess and flew off with her through the air. The boy wanted to set out after them at once, but the king would not let him, because he had no one else left now that his daughter was gone. Still, for all the king's orders and all the king's prayers, the boy would not stay. He changed into a falcon and sped off. By now they were out of sight, but he remembered the mysterious crag where he had rested during his first flight. He swooped down and settled there, changed into an ant and crept through a chink in the rock. After crawling along a while, he came to a door that was locked. He knew how to get through it, as he could creep in through the keyhole. And the next thing he saw was a strange princess lousing a big troll with three heads.

"This must be the right way," the boy thought to himself, for he had heard that the king had lost two other daughters whom the trolls had carried off. "Maybe I can find the second daughter too," he said to himself, and crept through the keyhole of the next door. There sat another strange princess lousing a big troll with six heads. And then he crept through another keyhole, and there sat the youngest princess lousing a big troll with nine heads. He crawled up the calf of her leg and pinched her. And she knew it was the lad wanting to speak to her, and so she asked the big troll for leave to go outside. When she came out, the boy appeared in his own shape and he told her to ask the big troll whether she would ever be able to go home to her father again. Then he became an ant and settled on her foot, and the princess went in and began lousing the big troll once more.

After a while she became lost in thought. "You are forgetting to louse me," said the troll. "What are you wondering about?"

"Oh, I'm wondering whether I shall ever leave here and return to my father's house," said the princess.

"No, you never will," said the big troll, "not unless someone finds the grain of sand that lies under the ninth tongue in the ninth head of the dragon to whom your father sent tribute. But no one will find it. If that grain of sand comes over this rock, all the trolls will burst and the rock will become a golden castle and the lake will turn into fields and meadows."

As soon as he heard this, the boy crept out again through all the keyholes and up through the crack in the rock. There he became a falcon and flew to where the dragon lay. And he searched until he found the grain of sand under the ninth tongue in the ninth head, and off he flew with it. But when he reached the lake, he was so weary that he had to sink down and rest on a stone by the shore. And while he was sitting there, he dozed just for a moment and at that moment the grain of sand fell from his beak down on the sandy shore. He had to search for three days before he found it again. But when he found it, he sped off to the crag with it and dropped it through the crack in the rock. Then all the trolls burst, the crag split asunder and a golden castle appeared, the fairest castle in all the world, and the lake changed into the most beautiful fields and the greenest meadows you could wish to see. And so they all returned to the king's dwelling, where there was no end of rejoicing. The boy and the youngest princess were made husband and wife, and there were revels throughout the kingdom for seven whole weeks to celebrate their wedding. And if they did not fare well, I only hope that you may fare better!

RUMBLE-MUMBLE
GOOSE-EGG

Once there were five women reaping in a field, and each one was childless and wanted a child of her own. All of a sudden they came upon a huge goose-egg as big as a man's head.

"I saw it first!" said one.

"I saw it just as soon as you did!" shouted another.

"By cripes, I mean to have it. I was the one that saw it first!" swore a third. And they went on squabbling over the egg and were ready to tear each other's hair.

In the end they agreed to keep it all five of them and sit on it in goose fashion and hatch out the gosling. The first one sat there for a week like a broody goose and had an easy time of it and did no work at all, while the others had to toil hard to feed themselves and her too. Then one of them cursed her for being so lazy.

"You couldn't twitter till you'd been in the egg a while yourself!" said the one who was brooding. "But in this egg at least there's something human, for it seems to be mumbling 'Herring and gruel and porridge and milk' over and over again," she said. "And now you can sit on it for a week, and we can take it in turns to feed you."

After the fifth woman had been sitting there brooding for a week, she could hear beyond doubt that there was a creature inside the egg shouting for 'Herring and gruel and porridge and milk,' and so she picked a hole in the eggshell. But instead of a gosling there burst forth a human child as ugly as could be with a big head and a little body. And his first cry on coming out of the egg was 'Herring and gruel and porridge and milk!' So they called him Rumble-Mumble Goose-Egg.

Though he was such an ugly fellow, they were all fond of him at first. But in no time he became so greedy that he ate

up all the food they had. Whenever they made a dish of gruel
or a pot of porridge that they thought would satisfy the six of
them, the youngster tipped it up and gulped down the lot. Then
they did not want to keep him any longer. "I haven't had a
decent feed since that blasted imp crawled out of his shell!"
said one of them. And when Rumble-Mumble Goose-Egg heard
the others complain too, he told them he was ready to leave;
if they could do without him, he could do without them. And
off he went.

He walked far until he came to a farm surrounded by stony
land. There he went in and asked for service. It seemed they
were in need of a labourer, and the old gaffer told him to clear
stones from the fields. And Rumble-Mumble Goose-Egg picked
up the stones. He collected big ones that made up several cart-
loads each, and he put the whole lot, both big and small, in
his pockets. He finished the job soon enough and went back
to find out what he was to do next.

"Clear away the stones from the field," said the farmer. "You
can't tell me you've finished when you've hardly begun."

But Rumble-Mumble Goose-Egg emptied his pockets and
threw all the stones in a heap. When the farmer saw that he

had done the work already, he felt he ought to watch his step with such a strong man and told him he had better come in and have something to eat. This suited Rumble-Mumble down to the ground, and he cleaned up the meal prepared for the household and the servants and still he had not had half enough.

There was nobody to match him as a worker, but there was nobody to match him as an eater either; feeding him was like pouring water through a sieve, thought the old gaffer. "A worker like that could eat a poor farmer out of house and home in three shakes of a lamb's tail," he said to himself.

He had no more work for him. It was best for him to go to the king's farm.

Rumble-Mumble Goose-Egg went off to the king and was taken on at once. On that farm there was food and work enough. He was to run errands and help the maids to carry wood and water and do other odd jobs.

He asked what he was to do first.

He could start by splitting up a bit of firewood, they said.

Rumble-Mumble Goose-Egg set to work and split and chopped and sent the splinters flying. In a jiffy he had chopped up all the wood he could find, firewood and timber and wood set aside for planks and tools, and when he had finished he came along and asked what they wanted him to do next.

"Finish chopping the wood," they said.

"There isn't any more," said Rumble-Mumble.

There must be more, thought the bailiff, and he went and took a look at the woodshed. But Rumble-Mumble Goose-Egg had chopped up the lot and made firewood of the planks and timber logs. The bailiff said that this was a disgrace and that he would not get a bite to eat till he had been to the forest and felled as much timber as he had split up into firewood.

Rumble-Mumble Goose-Egg ran down to the forge and got the smith to help him make an axe of five hundredweight of iron. And so he went off to the forest and cleared it. He cut down mast-timber and beam-timber of spruce and pine, everything he could find, in the king's forest and in the neighbouring forest as well. He left the tops and branches on and all the trees looked as if they had been swept down by a whirlwind. Then he piled a mighty load on the sledge and harnessed all the horses in front. But they could not make it budge, and as he tugged at the bridle to get the load moving he pulled all their heads off. So he tossed the horses out of the shafts and drew the load home himself.

When he reached the king's dwelling, the king and his forester were standing in the porch waiting to have a word with him about the way he had treated the forest, for the forester had been along there and seen it for himself. But as soon as Rumble-Mumble Goose-Egg came home dragging half the forest behind him, the king grew vexed and alarmed and thought he had better be cautious with such a strong man.

"You're a crack worker," said the king, "but how much do you eat at a time? You must be hungry now."

There went twelve tubs of meal to a portion of porridge for him, said Rumble-Mumble Goose-Egg. Though once he made an end of that, there was no need to feed him for a while.

It took some time to make as much porridge as this. In the meantime he had to bring in a load of wood for the cook. He stacked the whole wood-pile on a sledge, but as he was pulling it through the door he was a bit rough again. The wall timbers were all pushed askew, the corners slipped out of joint, and the whole house nearly fell down. When the dinner was just about ready, they sent him to call in the men. He shouted so loud that the hills echoed all around, but he thought the men were too slow in coming. So he had a scrap with them and knocked the life out of twelve.

"He knocked the life out of twelve," said the king, "and he eats much more than twelve times twelve. But how much work do you do, my boy?"

"Oh, much more than twelve times twelve," said Rumble-Mumble.

After he had had his dinner, he was sent to the barn to thresh corn. He lifted the ridge-pole off the roof to use as a flail, and when the roof started collapsing he took a giant spruce with all its branches on and put it along the ridge of the roof instead. And then he threshed grain and straw and hay all together. This did not turn out well, for both corn and chaff were whirled through the air and spread like a cloud over all the farm.

When he had almost got the threshing done, an enemy invaded the country and the king was at war. So the king told him to take some men with him and march against the army and meet them in battle, as the king was sure the enemy would kill him. No, he would not hear of any men losing their lives; he would fight alone, said Rumble-Mumble Goose-Egg.

All the better, thought the king, the sooner I'll be rid of him. But he had to have a good, strong club.

They sent for the smith, and he forged a club of two hundred-weight. Rumble-Mumble Goose-Egg said it was good enough to crack nuts with. So the smith forged a club of five hundred-weight, and Rumble-Mumble Goose-Egg said it was good enough to sole shoes with. The smith said it was the biggest job his men could do. And so Rumble-Mumble Goose-Egg went down to the forge himself and made a club of two tons, and it took a hundred men to turn it on the anvil. Rumble-Mumble Goose-Egg thought he could make do with this. Then he had to have a knapsack, and they made one out of fifteen oxhides and packed it with food, and off he tramped down the hill with his sack on his back and his club on his shoulder.

When he came within sight of the enemy, they sent a messenger to ask whether he was ready for battle.

"Wait till I've had a bite to eat," said Rumble-Mumble Goose-Egg. And he sat down on the ground behind his big knapsack and began his meal.

But the enemy could not wait. They started firing at once, and the bullets showered down on him like hailstones.

"I can do without all this chicken-feed," said Rumble-Mumble Goose-Egg and took out another helping. Both lead and steel bounced off him, and his knapsack gave cover like a rampart.

And so they started throwing grenades and shooting cannon-balls. He winced each time one touched him.

"There's no need to tickle me," he said. But then he got a grenade stuck in his throat.

"Ugh!" he said and spat it out. And next there came a chain-shot that cut through his butter-box, and then another chain-shot carried off a sandwich he was holding in his hand.

Then he got angry and jumped up and seized his big club and drummed it on the ground. And he asked them if they meant to keep on blowing the bread out of his mouth with their pea-shooters. And he beat upon the ground so the hills and mountains trembled and the enemy were scattered like chaff. And that was the end of that war.

When he came back again and asked for more work, the king grew pale, for this time he had hoped to be rid of him. The only thing he could think of was to send him to hell.

"Go off to Old Nick and collect the rent," he said. And off went Rumble-Mumble Goose-Egg with his sack on his back and his club on his shoulder and he made a quick journey of it. But when he got there, Old Nick was busy hearing the catechism for confirmation. There was no one at home but his mother, and she said she had never heard of any rent owing and he had better come back later.

"Tomorrow, I suppose!" he said, knowing it was all nonsense. He made it clear that once he was there he meant to stay until he got the rent and he had plenty of time to wait. But after he had eaten his meal, time began to drag. So he called to get the rent from the devil's mother again and told her she had to pay up straight away.

She refused point blank. She would no more budge than the great pine, she said. And that stood outside the gate of hell and fifteen men could scarcely put their arms around it. But Rumble-Mumble darted up to the top of the pine and bent and twisted it like a willow wand and asked her whether she would pay the rent now.

She dared not do otherwise and in a trice she found as many coins as Rumble-Mumble could carry in his sack. He took the rent and ran off towards home, and no sooner had he left than Old Nick came back. When he heard that Rumble-Mumble had made off with a big sack of money, he stopped first to wallop his mother and then he set out to catch up with him. And he

soon drew near, for he had no load and could fly through the
air whenever he chose, whereas Rumble-Mumble had to keep to
the ground with his heavy sack. But as Old Nick came hurrying
at his heels, he put a spurt on and raced along as fast as he could,
brandishing his club to keep him off. And so they ran on, with
Rumble-Mumble holding the handle tight and Old Nick grabbing
at the head of the club, until they came to a deep valley. There
Rumble-Mumble leapt from one mountain top to the other, and
Old Nick flew after him in such a rush that he dashed blindly
against the club and tumbled down into the valley and broke off
his foot. And there he lay.

"Here's your rent," said Rumble-Mumble Goose-Egg when
he reached the king's dwelling. And he tossed the sack at the
king's feet and the porch shook with the crash.

The king thanked him and made a fine speech and promised
him a rich reward and a safe journey home if he wished. But
Rumble-Mumble Goose-Egg only wanted more work.

"What do you want me to do next?" he asked.

The king scratched his head and then told him to go to the big troll who had stolen his grandfather's sword and who lived in the castle by the sea that no one dared approach.

Rumble-Mumble packed some bundles of food in his knapsack and off he went again. And he travelled a long, long way, across forests and mountains and wild hills, until he came to some tall rocks that were the home of the troll that had taken the king's grandfather's sword.

But the troll was nowhere to be seen and the rocks were shut and he could not find a way in.

Then he fell in with some quarrymen from a mountain farm who were quarrying stone in this rocky country. They had never had such help before. He broke up the mountain-face and split the rocks and sent boulders as big as houses toppling down. But when it was time for him to rest and have his dinner, he went to open one of his bundles and found it had all been eaten up.

"I've a good appetite myself," said Rumble-Mumble, "but whoever has been here has a better one. He has swallowed the bones as well."

So the first day passed, and on the second things were no better. On the third day he set out to break stones again and took the third bundle with him, but this time he lay down behind it and pretended to be asleep.

All of a sudden the mountain opened and out came a troll with seven heads and began gobbling the food in his bundle.

"Now I can have a good tuck in," said the troll.

"That's still to be settled!" said Rumble-Mumble, and he struck him with his club and knocked off his seven heads.

Then he went inside the mountain the troll had come from, and there he found a horse eating from a tub of red-hot embers and behind it was a tub of oats.

"Why don't you eat the oats?" said Rumble-Mumble Goose-Egg.

"Because I can't turn round," said the horse.

"I can turn you round," said Rumble-Mumble.

"I'd rather you tore off my head," said the horse.

He did so, and the horse became a fair young man. He told him he had been bewitched and changed into a horse by the troll. And he helped him find the sword that the troll had hidden at the bottom of the bed, and in the bed the troll's mother lay snoring away.

They set out homewards across the sea and when they had left the shore the troll's mother came after them. She could not catch them, and so she began drinking the water. And she drank so much that the level of the water sank. But she could not manage to drink up all the ocean, and in the end she burst.

As soon as they landed, Rumble-Mumble Goose-Egg sent word to the king asking him to fetch the sword. He sent four horses, but they could not move it. He sent eight and then he sent twelve, and still the sword stayed where it was and they could not make it stir an inch. So Rumble-Mumble Goose-Egg picked it up and carried it back himself.

The king could not believe his eyes when he saw Rumble-Mumble again. But he made a fine speech and promised him the earth and the moon. And when Rumble-Mumble wanted more work, he told him to go to the enchanted castle where no one dared stay and to make it his home until he had built a bridge over the sound so that people could get across. If he could do that, the king would reward him well and even give him his daughter, he said.

And Rumble-Mumble Goose-Egg said he would do it.

No one had ever returned from the spot alive. Those who had struggled to reach the castle lay slaughtered and torn to smithereens, and the king was certain he would have seen the last of him once he got him there.

But Rumble-Mumble set off. He took with him a sack of food and a good hard stump of pine, a small-axe, a wedge, and some kindling wood, and lastly the little pauper-boy from the king's farm.

When he reached the sound, the river was full of ice and roaring like a cataract. But he planted his feet firmly on the bottom and waded across and at last he was over on the other side.

79 After he had warmed himself by the fire and eaten his supper,

he was ready for a night's sleep. Then all of a sudden he heard a terrible din and it sounded as if the whole castle was being turned upside-down. And the door was swung wide open and all he could see was a gaping jaw as big as the doorway.

"Here's a mouthful for you! Try that!" said Rumble-Mumble and tossed the pauper-boy into the yawning gap. "But let me get a good look at you! Maybe we've met before."

They had met before, for it was Old Nick again. And they started playing cards, because he wanted to try and win back some of the money Rumble-Mumble had got out of his mother when he collected the king's rent. Somehow Rumble-Mumble kept winning, as he took care to mark the best cards. And after he won all the ready cash, Old Nick had to give Rumble-Mumble the gold and silver from the castle.

All at once the fire went out and they could not see to play.

"We'll have to cut some wood," said Rumble-Mumble. He struck the stump of pine with his axe and drove in the wedge, but the old log was gnarled and tough and would not split, though Rumble-Mumble prized and wrenched with his axe. "You're supposed to be strong," he said to Old Nick. "Spit on your hands and dig in your claws and let's see if you can wrench this log apart!" he said.

Old Nick got to work and dived his hands into the crack and wrenched as hard as he could. At that moment Rumble-Mumble Goose-Egg drove out the wedge and he had Old Nick caught in a tight spot. And then he tried out his axe-head on his back. Old Nick begged to be set free, but Rumble-Mumble Goose-Egg turned a deaf ear until he promised that he would never come and harry there again. And he also had to promise to build a bridge over the sound so that people could cross it at all times of the year and it was to be ready as soon as the ice melted.

"Those are hard terms," said Old Nick.

Still he had no choice. If he wanted to be free he had to make this promise. But he struck a bargain that he was to get the first soul that crossed the bridge. That soul was to be paid to him as toll.

80   Rumble-Mumble agreed to this, and Old Nick was set free

and sped off home. Rumble-Mumble Goose-Egg went to bed
to sleep on it all and he was still asleep late next day.

When the king came to see whether he had been chopped up
or just torn to pieces, he had to wade through gold and silver
before he could get to the bed. Sacks of it lay heaped along the
walls and in the bed Rumble-Mumble was snoring soundly.

"Heaven help me and my daughter!" he said, once he realised Rumble-Mumble was alive and kicking. Well, there was no denying that a splendid job had been done, he said; but there could scarcely be talk of any wedding until after the bridge had been built.

One fine day the bridge was all finished, and on it stood Old Nick waiting for his toll as promised in the bargain.

Rumble-Mumble Goose-Egg wanted to take the king with him to try out the bridge, but he did not like the idea. So he mounted a horse himself and swung up on the front of his saddle the enormous lump of a dairy-woman who kept the king's cows – she looked just like a huge stump of pine – and the bridge thundered as he rode across.

"Where is my toll? Where is the soul?" shouted Old Nick.

"In this lump of pinewood here! If you want it, spit on your hands and catch it!" said Rumble-Mumble Goose-Egg.

"Oh no, thanks! If she won't have me, I won't have her!" said Old Nick. "You've had me in a tight spot before and I'm not being caught again!" And in a flash he flew straight home to his old mother and has never been heard of since.

But Rumble-Mumble Goose-Egg hurried off to the king's farm to claim the reward that the king had promised. And when the king shillied and shallied and tried to go back on his word, Rumble-Mumble said he had better prepare a sizable sack of food and then he would collect his reward himself. The king gave orders for this to be done, and as soon as the sack was ready Rumble-Mumble took the king out to the threshold and gave him a good solid whack that sent him sailing up in the air. He hurled the sack of food after him so he should not go hungry, and unless they have come down again the king and his knapsack are still sailing along between heaven and earth this very day.